Use these stickers for the activities in the book

Page 2

Page 5

ee ee

Page 8

Page 7

ar ar
ar ar

Page 12

Page 11

p p p
p p

KU-943-043

the activities!

Well done!

Well done!

Well done!

Well done!

Well done!

Well done!

Well done!

Well done!

Page 11

pillow → picture → patchwork

Page 15

ou ou ou ou

Pages 16–17

a a a a a a a a

Page 19

sl sn sn st

Page 21

w w w w w

Page 22

f f f f f

Page 24

snack

garden

table apple

fork fire

coat

picture

mouse

Well done!

Well done!

Get Set Go Phonics

Snow White
and the Seven Dwarfs

Phonics Consultant: Susan Purcell

Illustrator: Natalia Moore

Concept: Fran Bromage

Miles Kelly

As you read aloud, focus on the b sound (as in born)

Once upon a time, a **b**eautiful **b**aby girl was **b**orn to a king and queen. They named her Snow White.

But sadly the queen died **b**efore the **b**aby was a year old.

Say the words as you spot each thing beginning with b.

Stick on their stickers.

2

baby

beard

boot

The king **m**arried again, but his new wife was **m**ean.

She had a **m**agic **m**irror, to which she would say,

"**M**irror, **m**irror on the wall, who is the fairest of them all?"

"**M**y lady, you are the fairest of them all," the **m**irror replied.

What a good try! Put a gold star here.

Sound out these words beginning with the **m** sound.

map   **m**oth   **m**ilk

moon   **m**arket   **m**onster

3

Focus on the
ee sound
(as in qu**ee**n)

The m**ea**n qu**ee**n always heard the same answer from the mirror.

But when Snow White was sixt**ee**n, the mirror replied,

"My qu**ee**n, you are very fair – but Snow White s**ee**ms to b**e** the fairest of them all."

Sound out these words with the **ee** sound.

b**ea**t   t**ea**m   cl**ea**n

d**ee**p   sl**ee**p   ch**ee**se   t**ee**th

4

See she never returns!

The qu**ee**n was gr**ee**n with envy. She ordered a huntsman to s**ee**k out Snow White and take her d**ee**p into the forest.

Use your stickers to **spell** some more words with the **ee** sound.

b**ea**n   h**ea**t   tr**ee**   s**ee**n

Point out the ar sound (as in arm) as you read

The huntsman took Snow White by the arm, but did her no harm. He told her to run far away.

Sound out these words with the ar sound.

part   star   market

sharp   cart   dark   garden

Al**ar**med, Snow White ran f**ar** into the wood.

She was st**ar**ting to feel tired, when she saw a ch**ar**ming cottage.

Use your stickers to **spell** some more words with the **ar** sound.

b**ar**n   p**ar**ty   f**ar**m   sm**ar**t

Snow White **t**apped on the door and **t**iptoed in. Everything inside was very **t**iny and **t**erribly **t**idy.

Say the words as you spot things beginning with t.

Stick on their stickers.

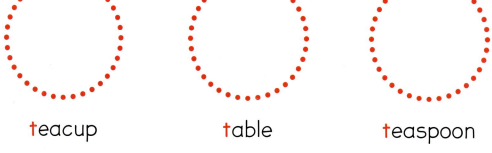

teacup

table

teaspoon

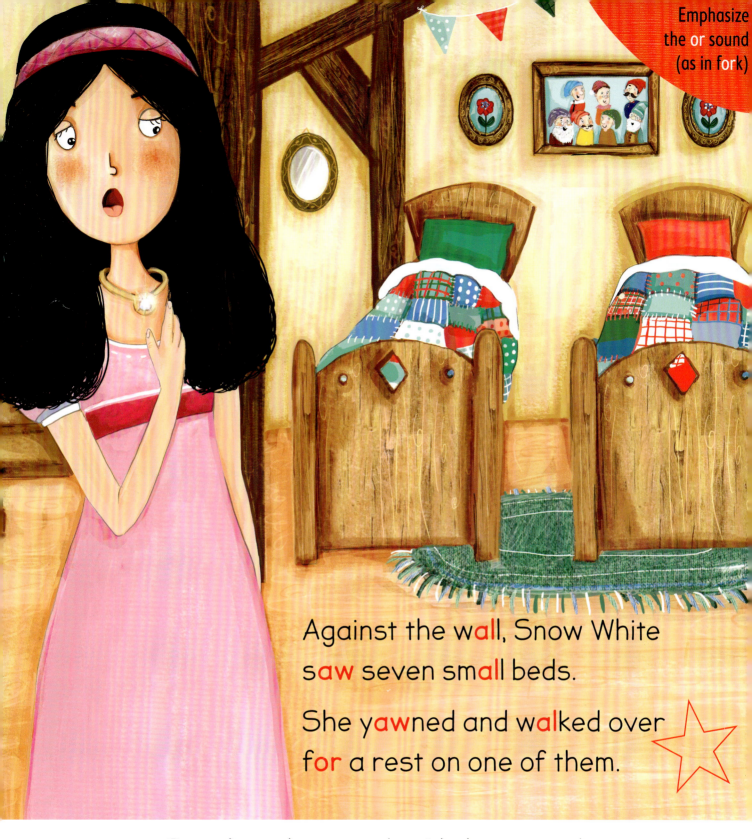

Emphasize
the or sound
(as in fork)

Against the wall, Snow White saw seven small beds.

She yawned and walked over for a rest on one of them.

Sound out these words with the **or** sound.

fork   short   hall   talk

chalk   crawl   draw

Hours later, when Snow White awoke, she wasn't alone.

She did not know she was in the home of seven dwarfs. They all spoke kindly to her.

Sound out these words, which all have the oa sound.

show   yellow   coat   boat

hole   rope   broke

"**P**erhaps you'd like to stay," said a dwarf in a **p**urple hat, **p**opping up near the bed.

Use your arrow stickers to **point** to some things that begin with **p**.

Use your stickers to **spell** some words beginning with the **p** sound.

pen   **p**ond   **p**ut   **p**ark   **p**ink

11

So, each day as the seven dwarfs set off for work Snow White fussed over them and made them sandwiches.

Say the words as you spot each thing with the s sound.

Stick on their stickers.

12

glasses

grass

dress

Meanwhile, one night the magic mirror told the evil queen that Snow White was still alive.

"You lie!" cried the queen with all her might.

Sound out these words, which all use the **ie** sound.

high   fight   light

pie   tie   ice   mile   time

13

The queen was so ann**oy**ed! Snow White was sp**oi**ling her plan to be the fairest in the land.

So, the queen p**oi**soned an apple, disguised her face and v**oi**ce, and set off to j**oi**n Snow White.

Sound out these words with the **oi** sound.

b**oy**　　t**oy**　　enj**oy**

oil　　c**oi**n　　s**oi**l　　p**oi**nt

14

She f**ou**nd Snow White safe and s**ou**nd in the dwarfs' h**ou**se.

"Apples for sale!" sh**ou**ted the queen, with a fr**ow**n.

Emphasize the ow sound (as in frown)

Use the stickers to **spell** some words with the ow sound.

ab**ou**t m**ou**nt h**ou**nd m**ou**se

The queen beg**a**n to eat one side of an **a**pple.

You can h**a**ve this one.

But it wasn't the b**a**d, poisoned part. The queen h**a**nded the **a**pple to Snow White.

Use your stickers to **spell** some words with the **a** sound.

ant   **a**dd   m**a**n   c**a**p   r**a**t

16

Snow White began to eat the poisoned side of the apple. After one bite, she fell down as if dead!

Use your stickers to **complete** the sentence with the **a** sound.

Snow White began to eat the apple.

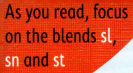

As you read, focus on the blends sl, sn and st

When the dwarfs returned, they were **st**artled to see **Sn**ow White lying on the ground. She lay as **st**ill as a **st**one.

Sound out these words, which have **sl**, **sn** and **st** blends.

slug   **sl**ipper   **sn**ap   **sn**eeze

stuff   **st**ep   **st**ory

18

The dwarfs **sn**atched up the apple and realised **Sn**ow White had been poisoned.

Stunned, they **sl**owly placed **Sn**ow White in a glass case, and **st**ood it in the woods.

Use your stickers to **spell** some words with the **sl**, **sn** and **st** blends.

slide   snack   snore   stung

One day, a **h**andsome prince rode past. As **h**e leant over to look at Snow White **h**e knocked the glass case.

The **h**orrible piece of apple flew out of **h**er mouth, and she opened **h**er eyes.

Say the names of the things with the **h** sound, as you spot them.

horse **h**air **h**ead

hedge **h**and

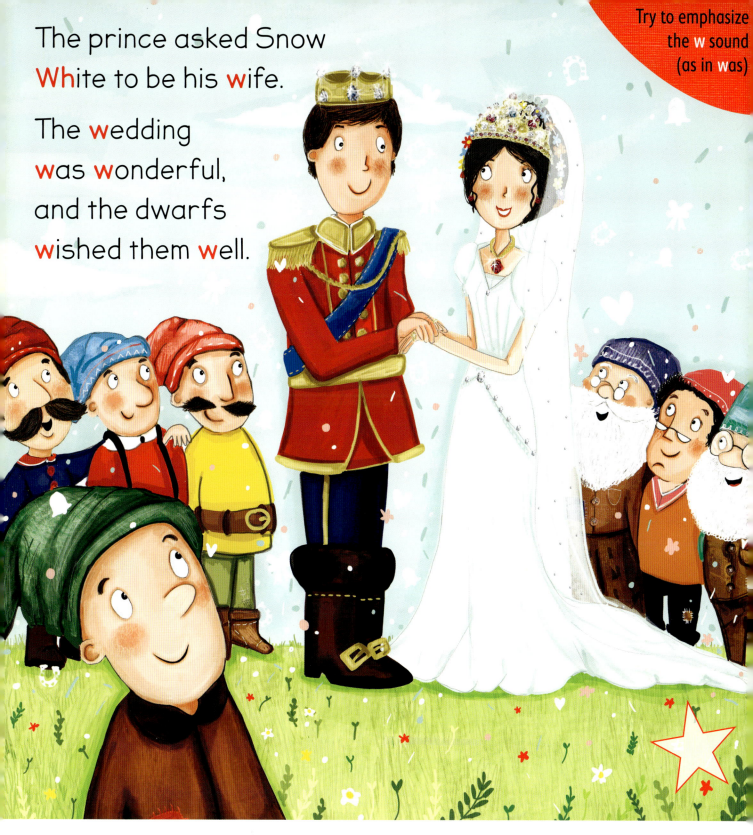

The prince asked Snow **Wh**ite to be his **w**ife.

The **w**edding **w**as **w**onderful, and the dwarfs **w**ished them **w**ell.

Try to emphasize the **w** sound (as in **w**as)

Use your stickers to **spell** these words, which all use the **w** sound.

wet   **w**ay   **w**on   **w**ish   **w**eb

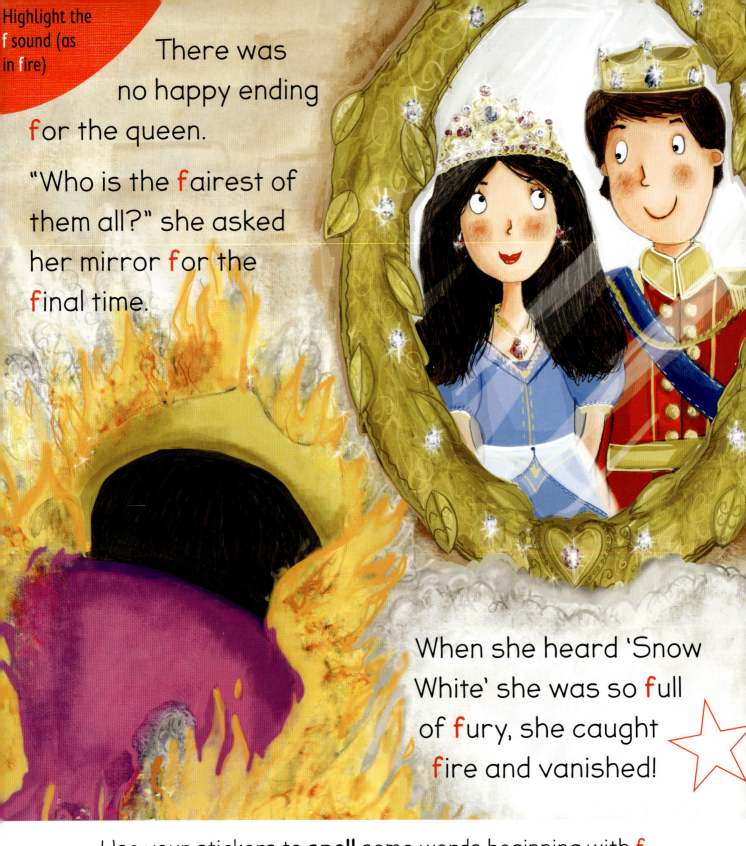

There was no happy ending for the queen.

"Who is the fairest of them all?" she asked her mirror for the final time.

When she heard 'Snow White' she was so full of fury, she caught fire and vanished!

Use your stickers to **spell** some words beginning with f.

fed   fish   fog   fast   fur

Ask your child to **retell** the story using these key sounds and story images.

ba**b**y

mirror

qu**ee**n

seven

cr**ie**d

po**i**soned

still

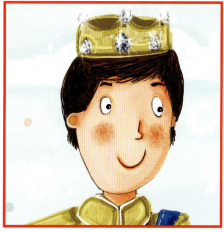
handsome

wedding

Use your stickers to **add** a word that matches
the red highlighted **sounds** on each line.

f**ar**   p**ar**t   f**ar**m

tidy   **t**iny   **t**eacup

sh**or**t   t**al**k   cr**aw**l

sn**ow**   kn**ow**   al**o**ne

pond   **p**ink   **p**illow

fr**ow**n   h**ou**se   sh**ou**t

ant   m**a**n   r**a**t

snore   **sn**eeze   **sn**ap

full   **f**ury   **f**ast

You've had fun with phonics! Well done.